CHRISTMAS GUITAR DUETS

Arranged by Mark Phillips

ISBN 978-1-7051-6826-4

HAL•LEONARD®

Visit Hal Leonard Online at
www.halleonard.com

World headquarters, contact:
Hal Leonard
7777 West Bluemound Road
Milwaukee, WI 53213
Email: info@halleonard.com

In Europe, contact:
Hal Leonard Europe Limited
1 Red Place
London, W1K 6PL
Email: info@halleonardeurope.com

In Australia, contact:
Hal Leonard Australia Pty. Ltd.
4 Lentara Court
Cheltenham, Victoria, 3192 Australia
Email: info@halleonard.com.au

CONTENTS

THE CHRISTMAS SONG
(Chestnuts Roasting on an Open Fire)

Music and Lyric by Mel Tormé and Robert Wells

*For all three-note chords, play top note on 3rd string.

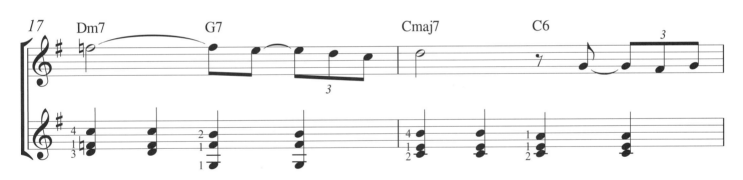

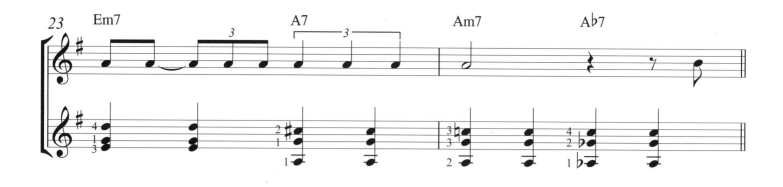

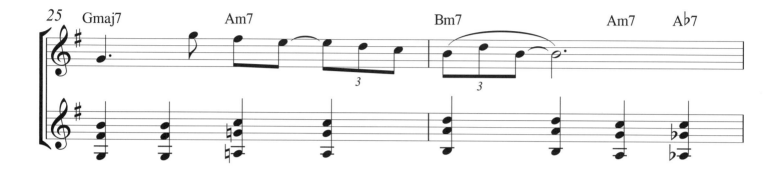

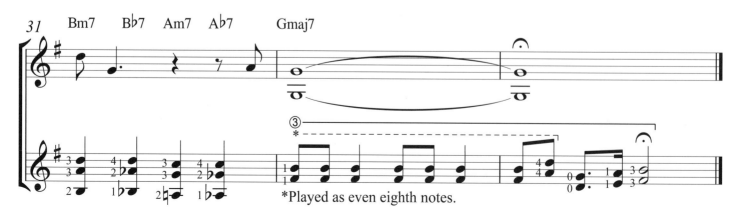

*Played as even eighth notes.

6

DECK THE HALL

Traditional Welsh Carol

Moderately fast

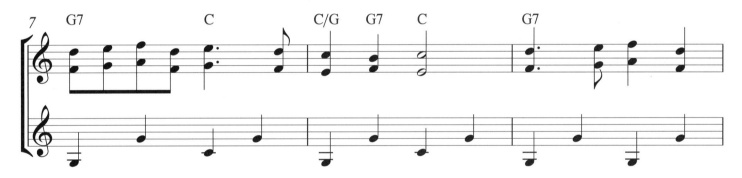

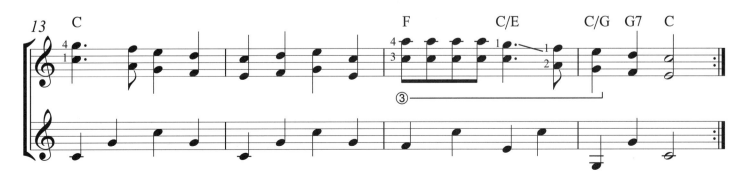

CHRISTMAS TIME IS HERE

from A CHARLIE BROWN CHRISTMAS

Words by Lee Mendelson
Music by Vince Guaraldi

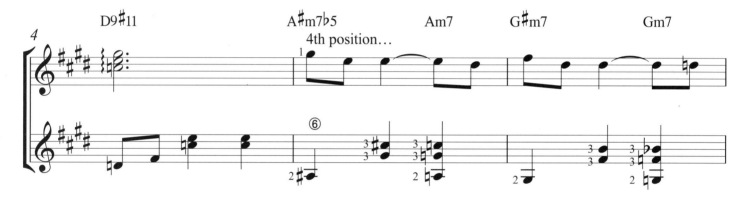

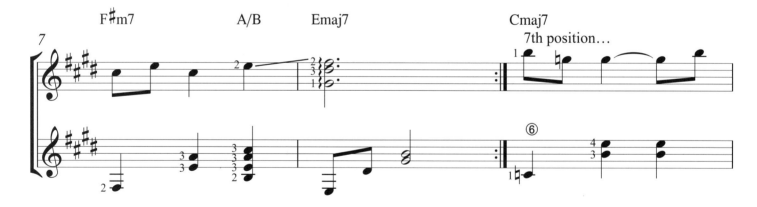

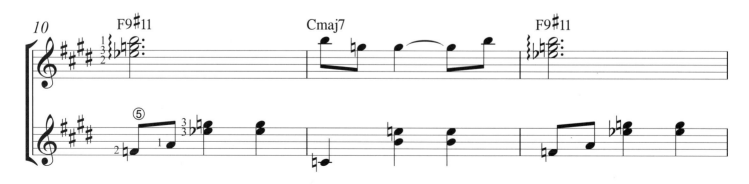

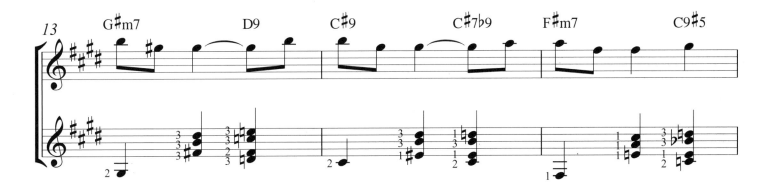

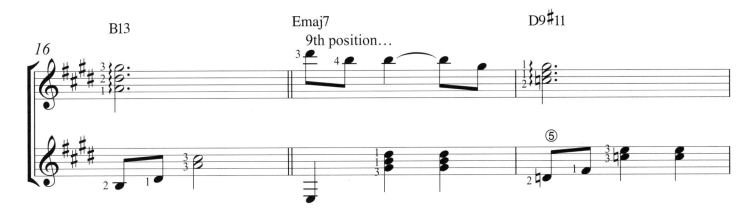

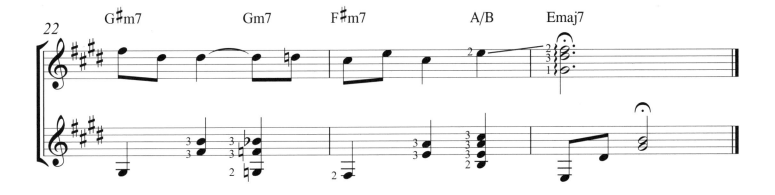

DO YOU HEAR WHAT I HEAR

Words and Music by Noel Regney and Gloria Shayne

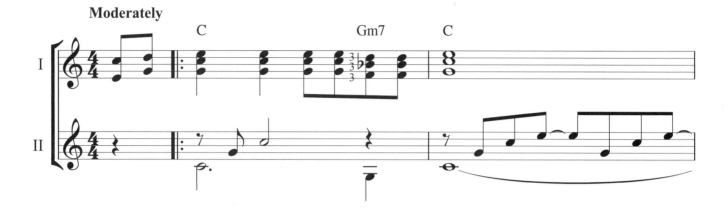

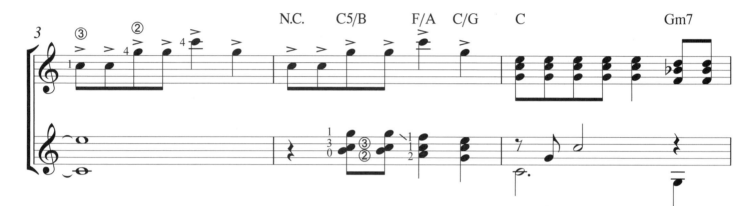

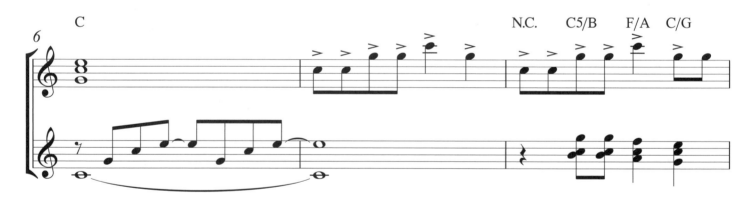

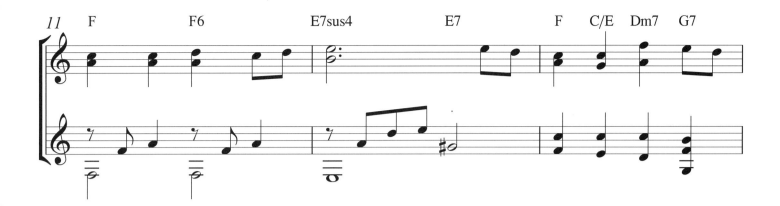

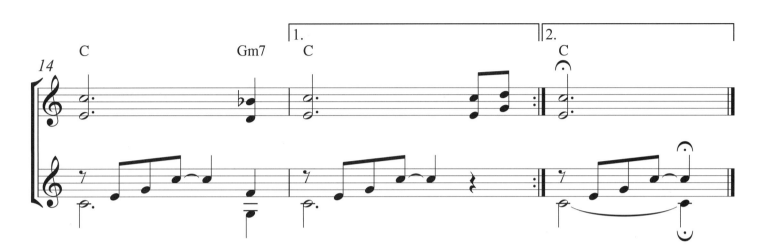

FELIZ NAVIDAD

Music and Lyrics by José Feliciano

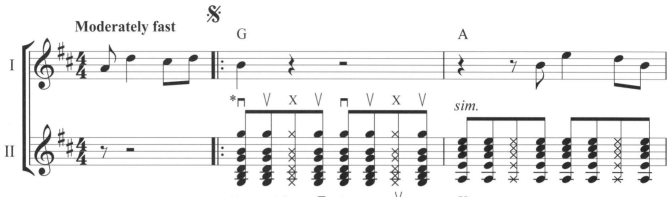

*Strum w/ fingers; □ = downstrum, V = upstrum, X = percussive mute (slap strings with R.H.)

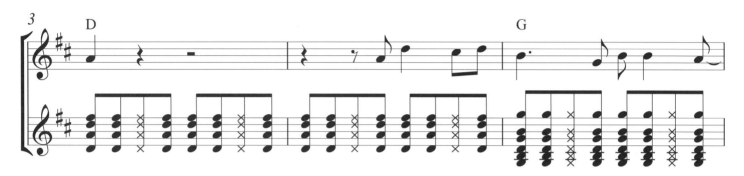

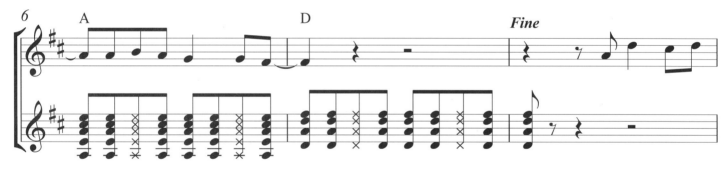

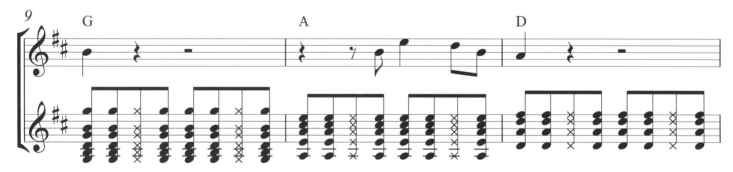

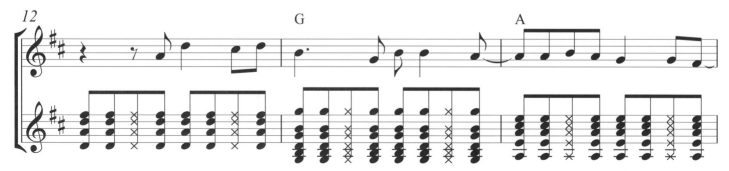

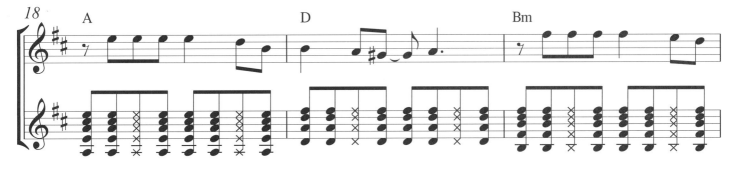

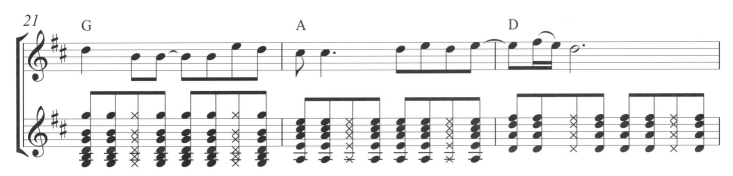

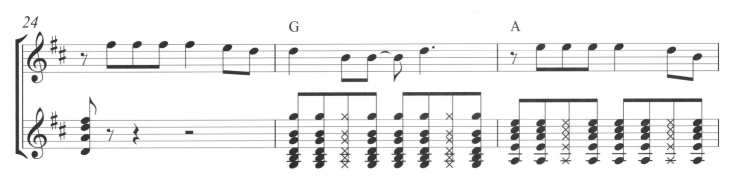

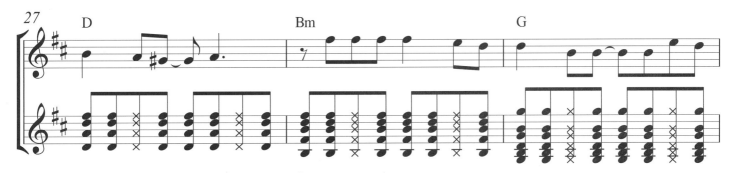

2nd time, D.S. al Fine

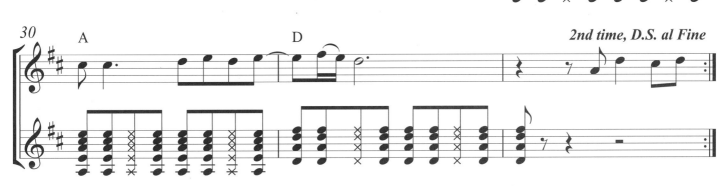

FROSTY THE SNOW MAN

Words and Music by Steve Nelson and Jack Rollins

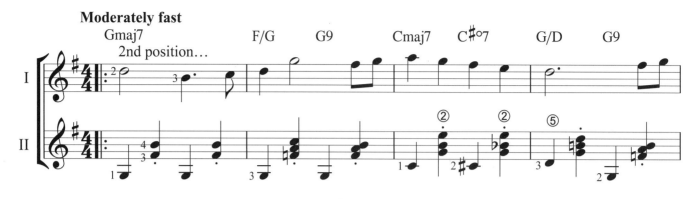

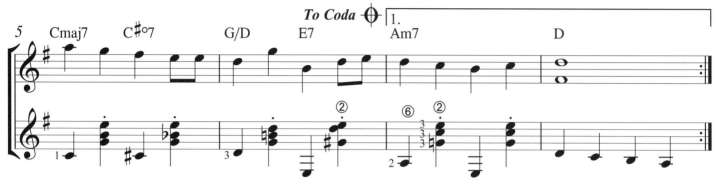

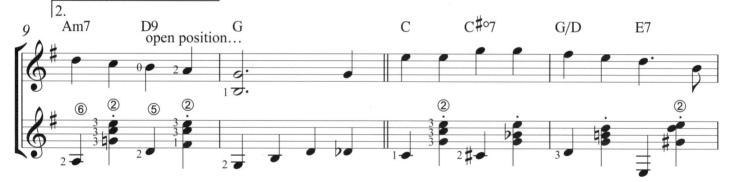

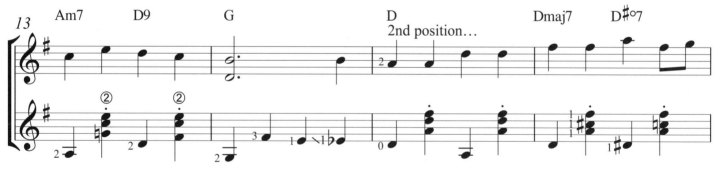

HAPPY XMAS
(War Is Over)
Written by John Lennon and Yoko Ono

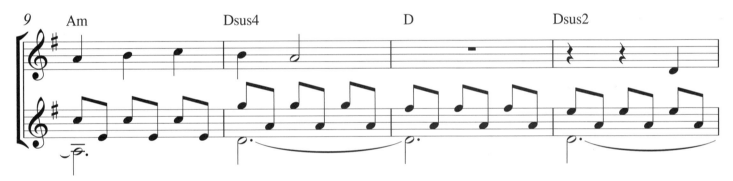

HAVE YOURSELF A MERRY LITTLE CHRISTMAS

from MEET ME IN ST. LOUIS

Words and Music by Hugh Martin and Ralph Blane

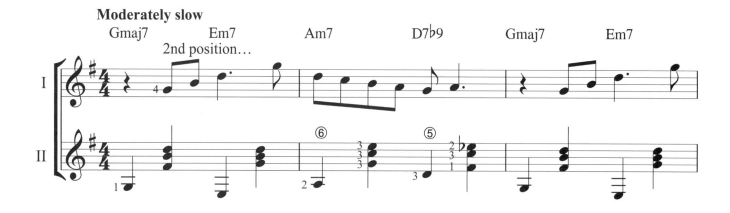

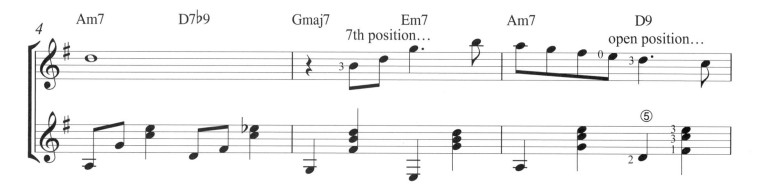

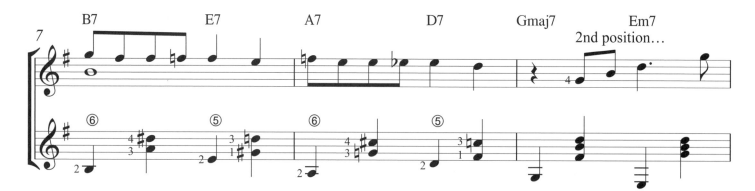

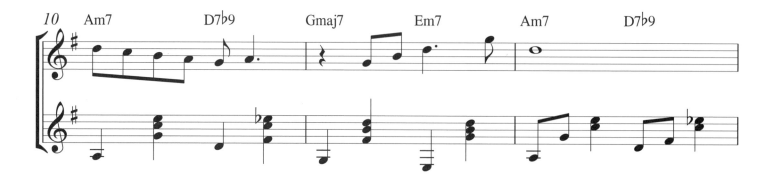

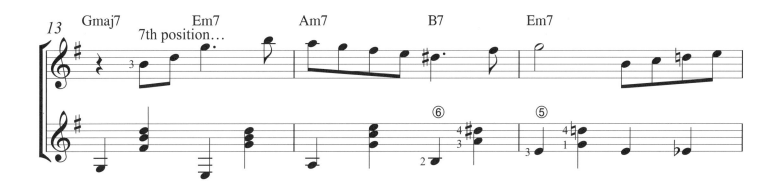

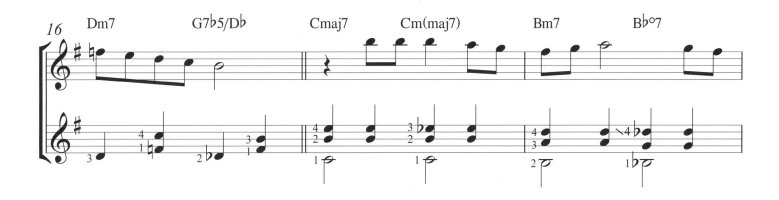

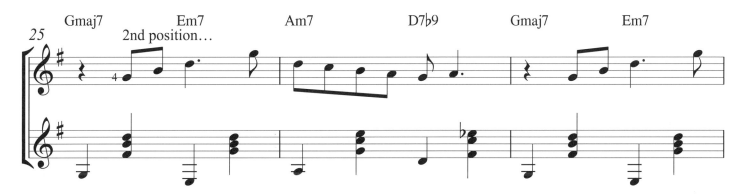

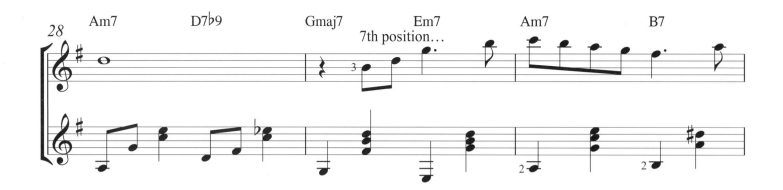

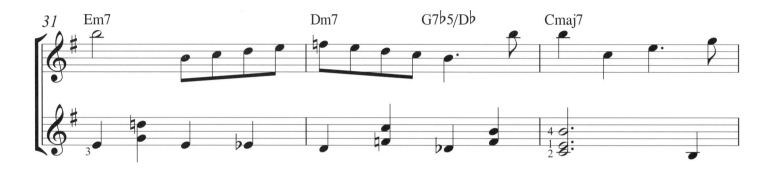

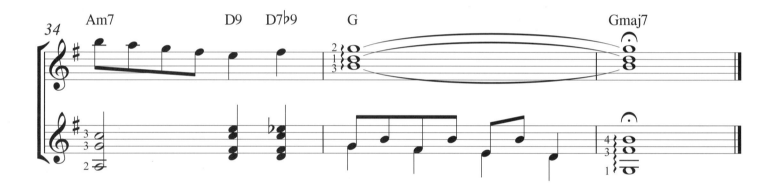

HERE COMES SANTA CLAUS
(Right Down Santa Claus Lane)

Words and Music by Gene Autry and Oakley Haldeman

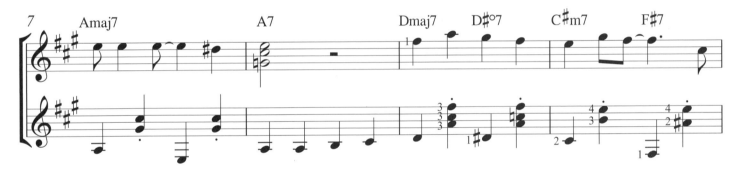

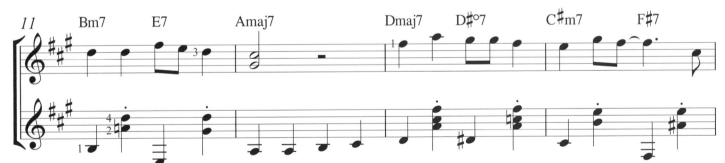

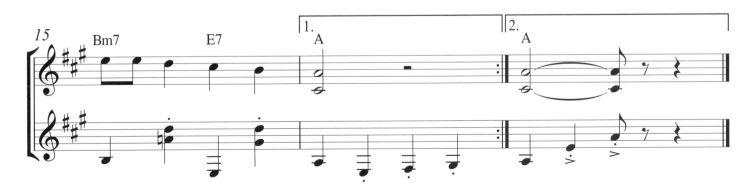

A HOLLY JOLLY CHRISTMAS

Music and Lyrics by Johnny Marks

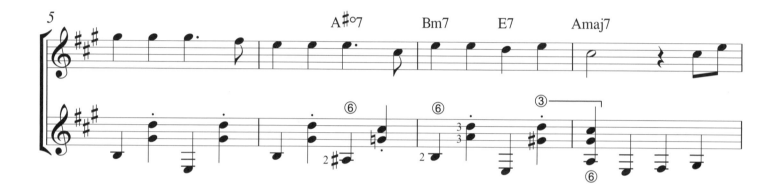

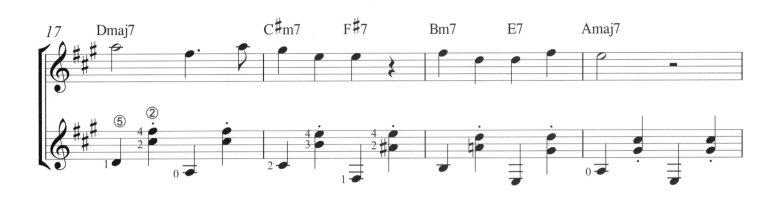

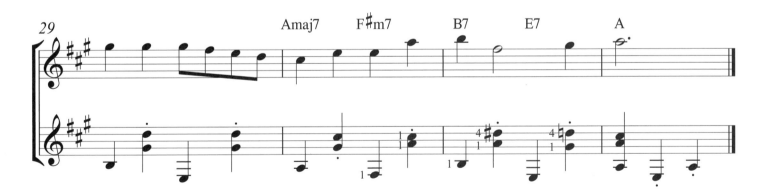

I'LL BE HOME FOR CHRISTMAS

Words and Music by Kim Gannon and Walter Kent

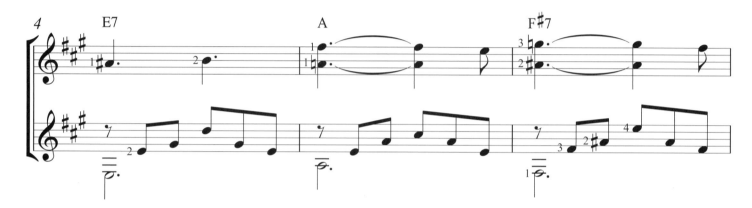

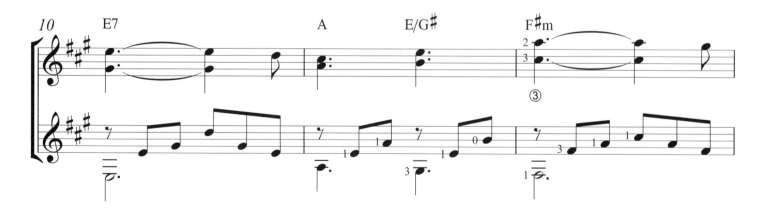

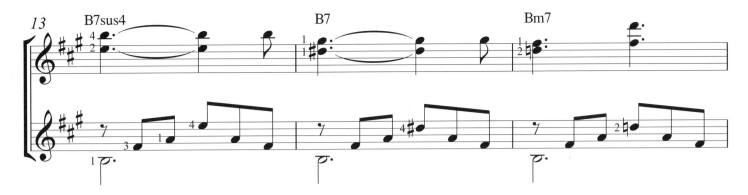

D.C. al Coda

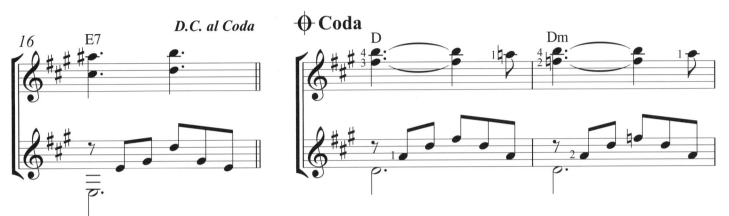

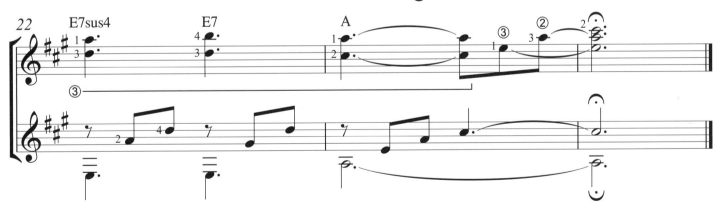

JINGLE BELL ROCK

Words and Music by Joe Beal and Jim Boothe

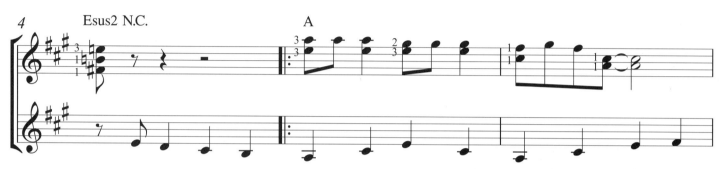

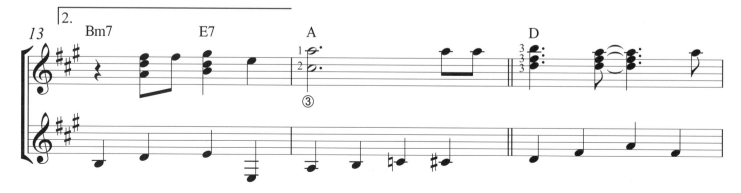

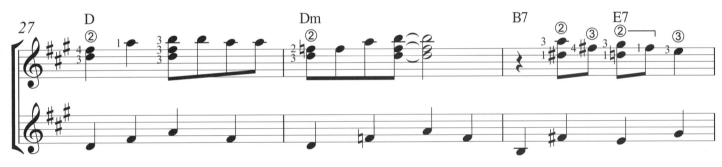

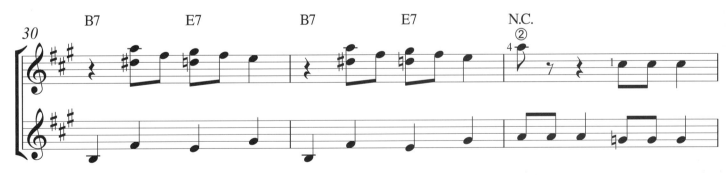

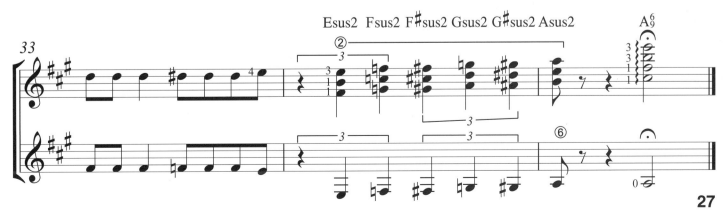

JINGLE BELLS

Words and Music by J. Pierpont

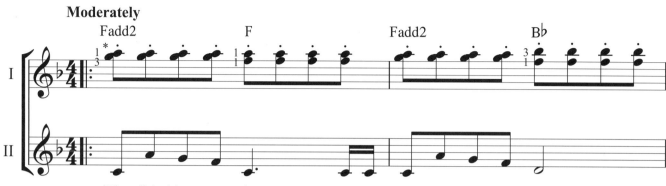

*Play all double stops on strings 2 & 3.

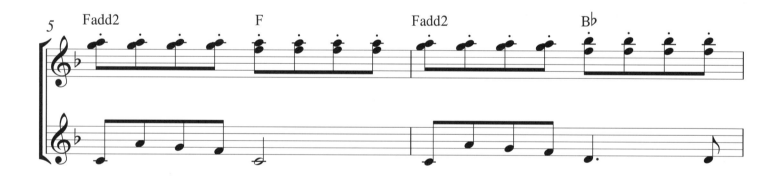

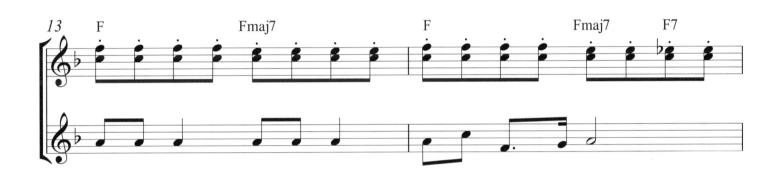

LAST CHRISTMAS

Words and Music by George Michael

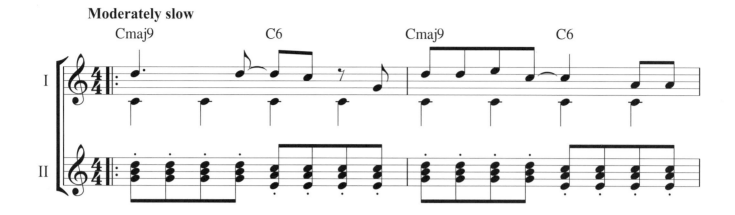

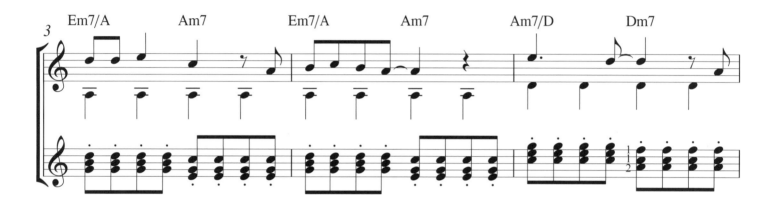

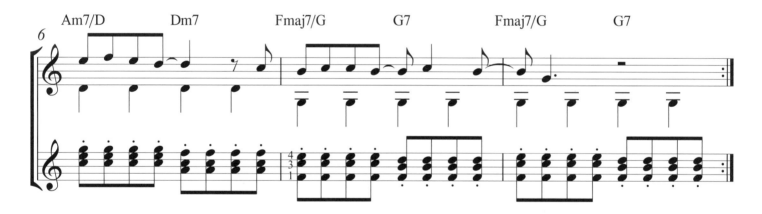

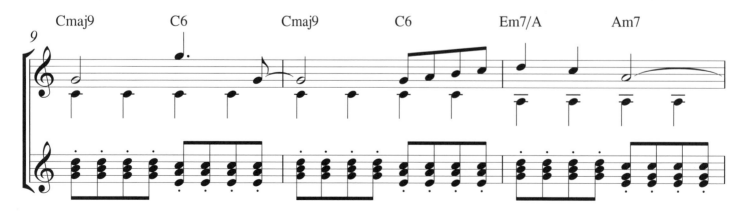

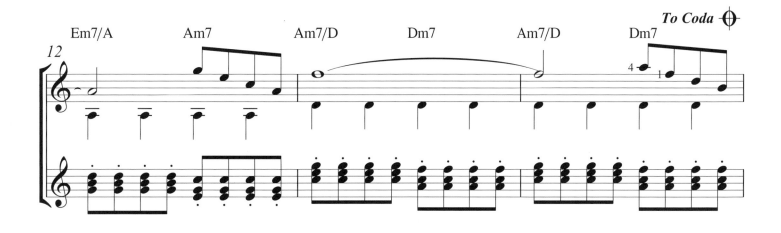

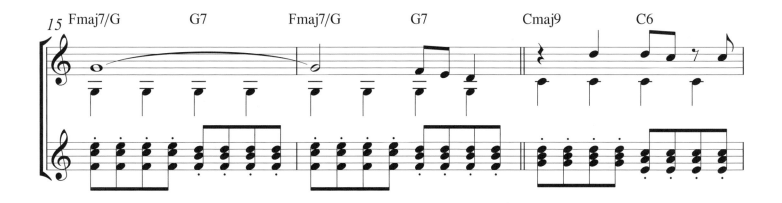

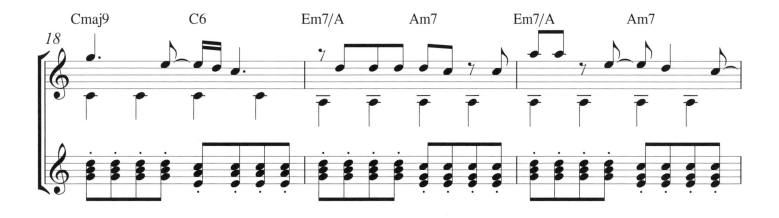

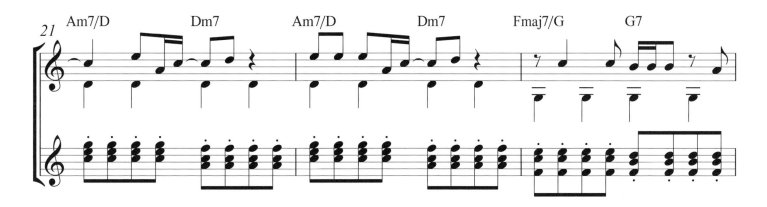

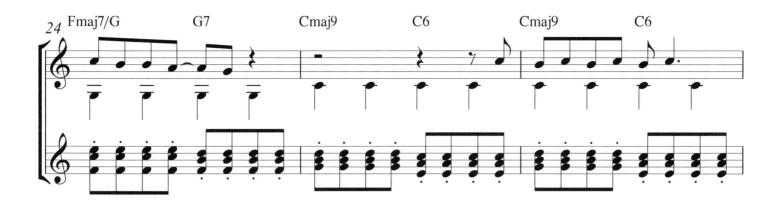

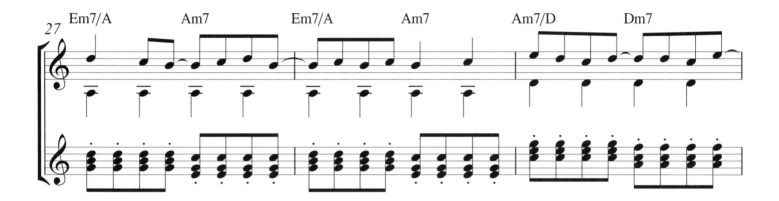

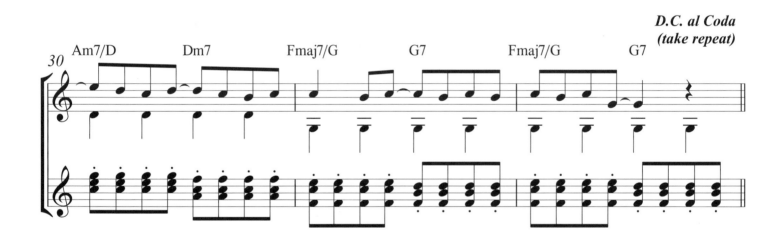

D.C. al Coda
(take repeat)

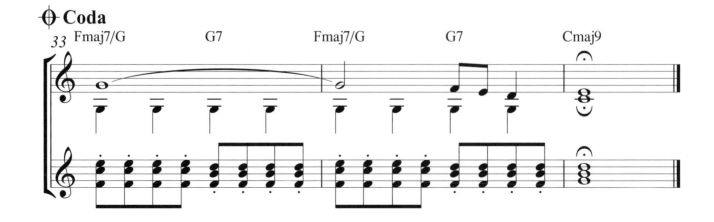

SLEIGH RIDE

Music by Leroy Anderson

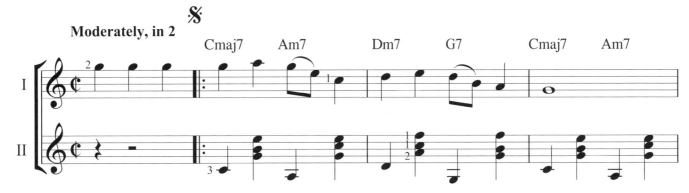

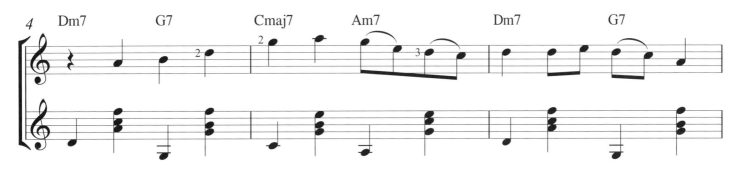

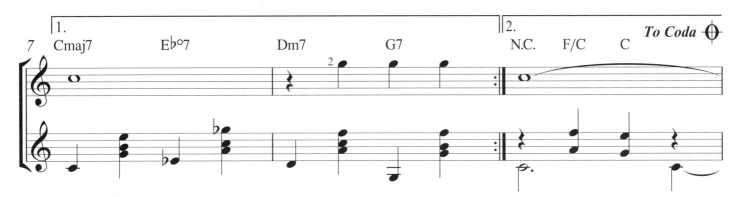

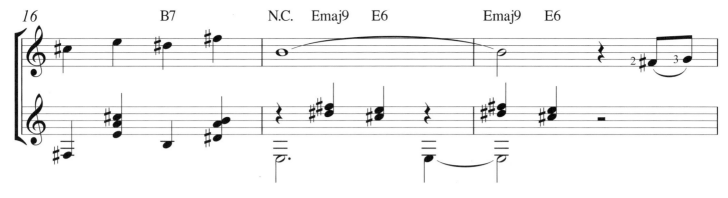

D.S. al Coda
(take repeat)

⊕ **Coda**

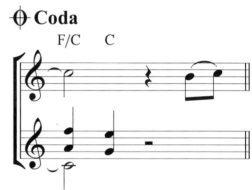

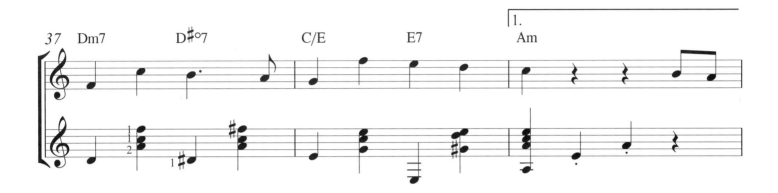

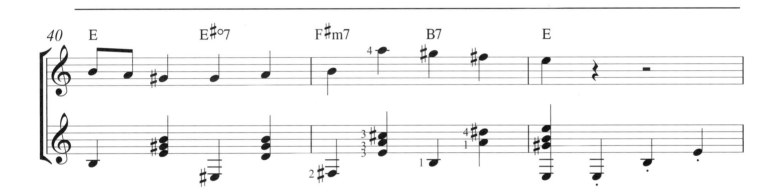

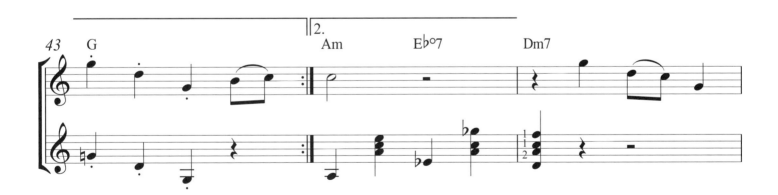

D.S. al Fine
(take repeat)

LET IT SNOW! LET IT SNOW! LET IT SNOW!

Words by Sammy Cahn
Music by Jule Styne

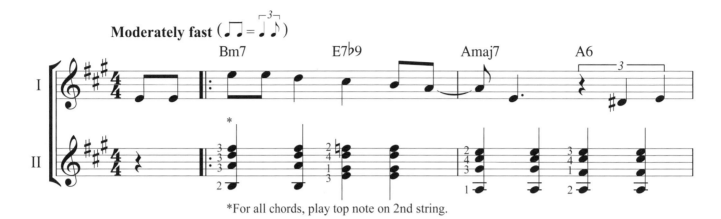

*For all chords, play top note on 2nd string.

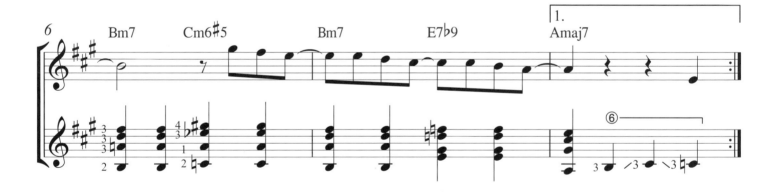

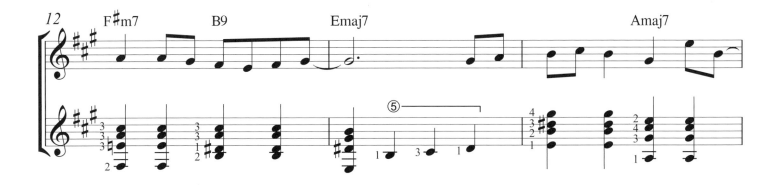

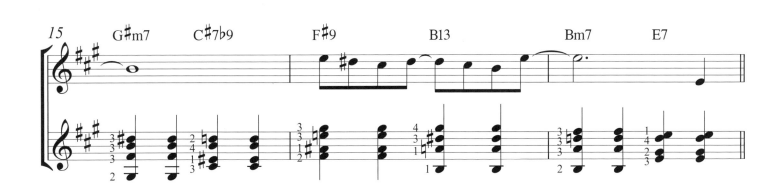

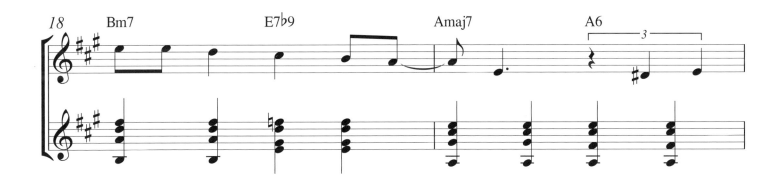

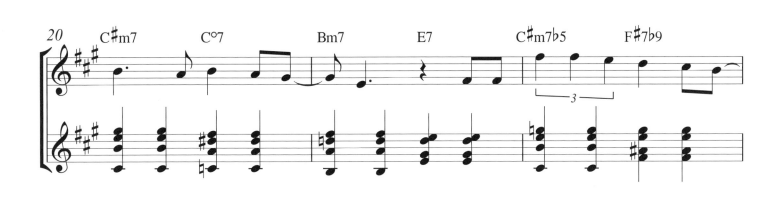

THE LITTLE DRUMMER BOY

Words and Music by Harry Simeone, Henry Onorati and Katherine Davis

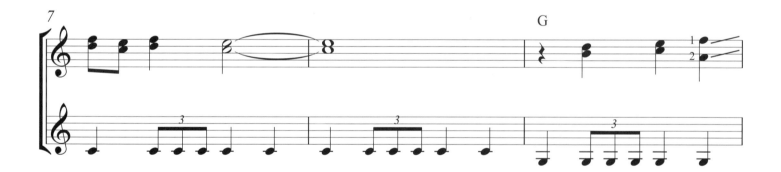

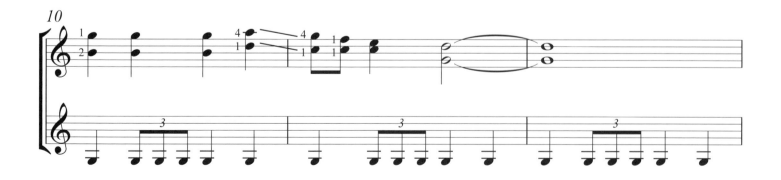

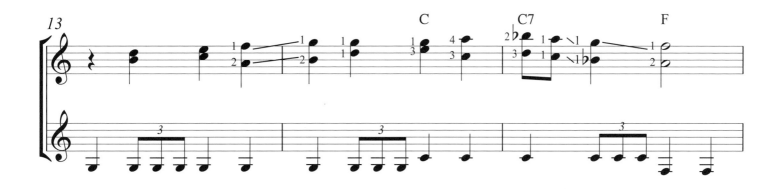

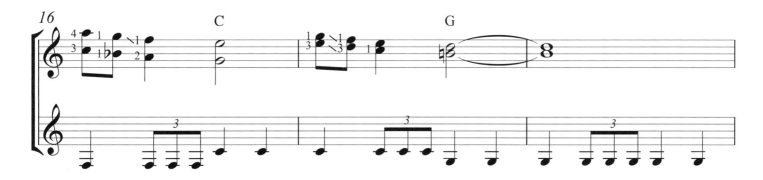

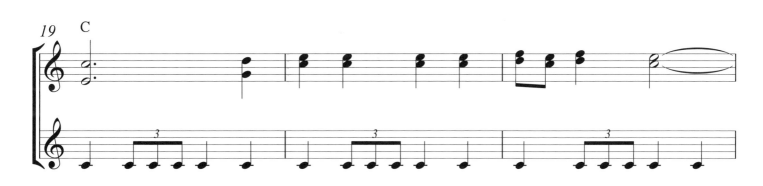

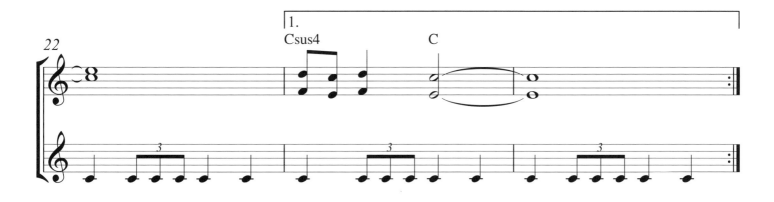

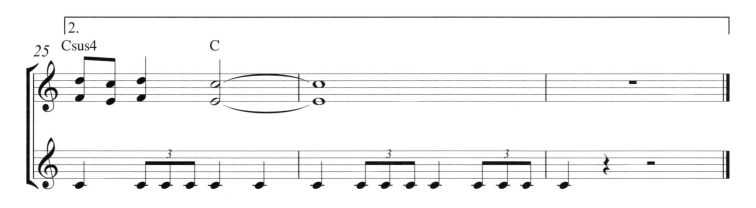

MARY, DID YOU KNOW?

Words and Music by Mark Lowry and Buddy Greene

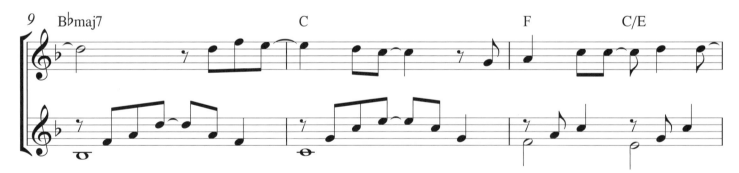

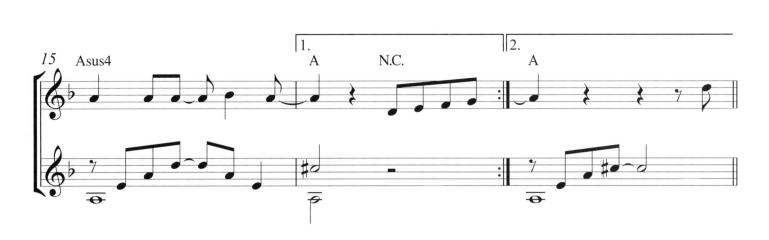

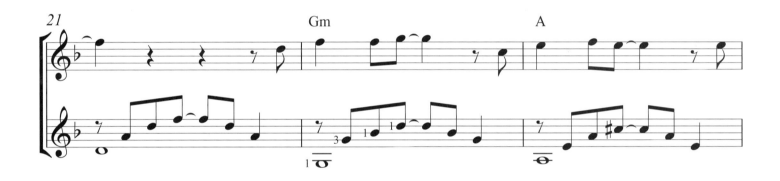

RUDOLPH THE RED-NOSED REINDEER

Music and Lyrics by Johnny Marks

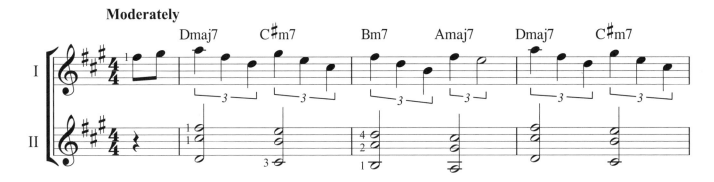

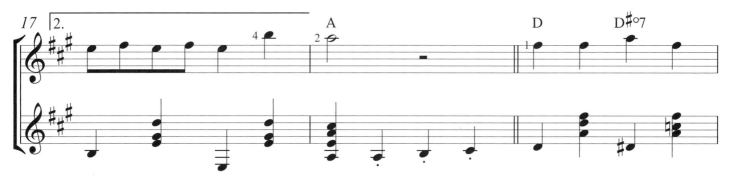

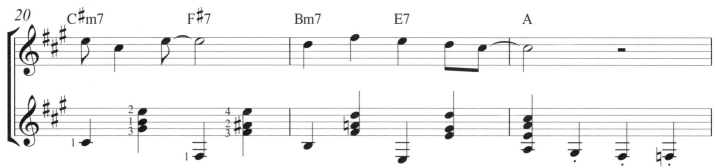

SANTA CLAUS IS COMIN' TO TOWN

Words by Haven Gillespie
Music by J. Fred Coots

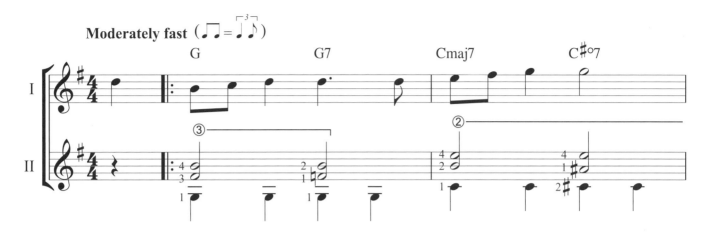

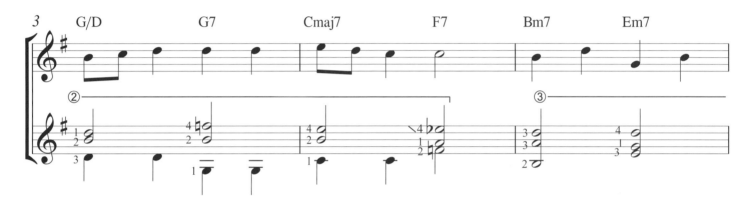

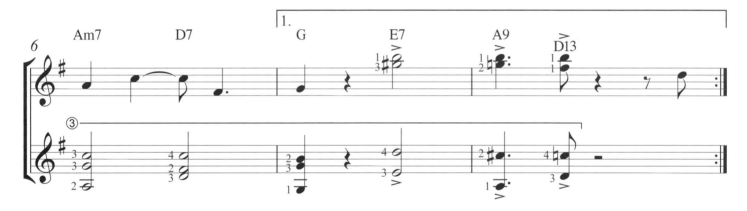

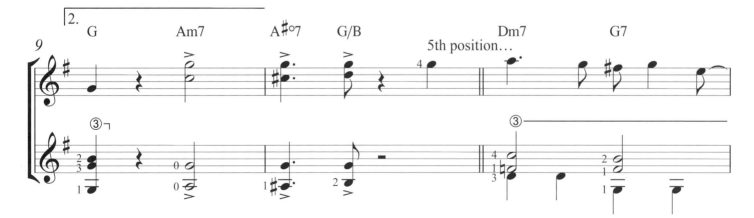

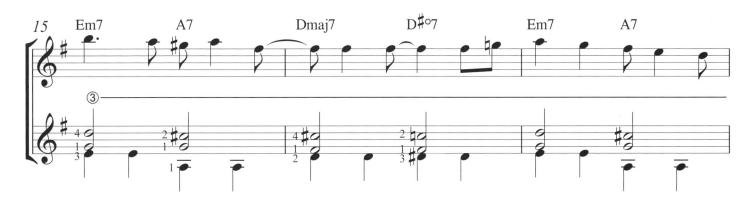

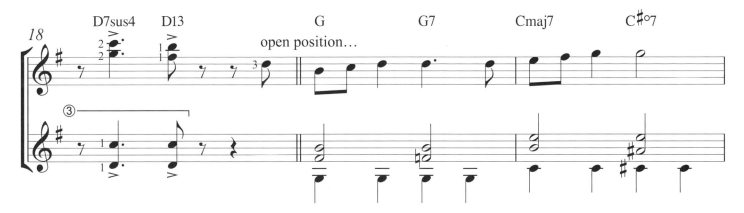

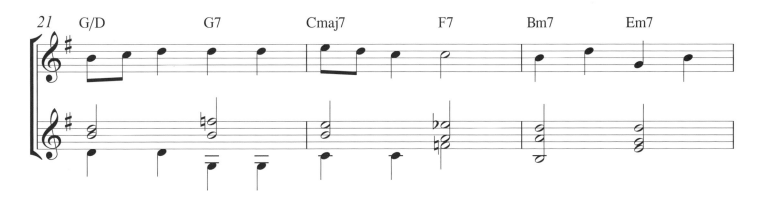

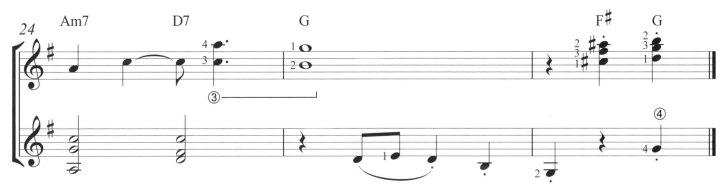

SILVER BELLS

from the Paramount Picture THE LEMON DROP KID

Words and Music by Jay Livingston and Ray Evans

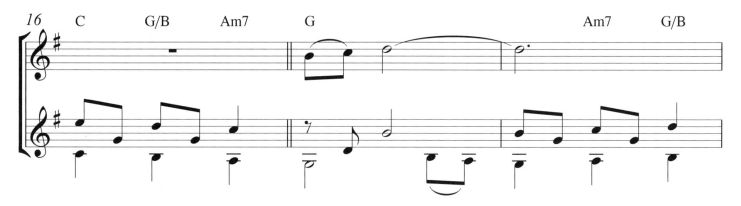

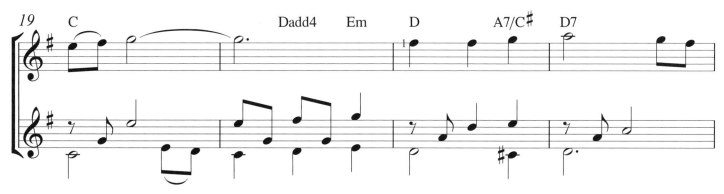

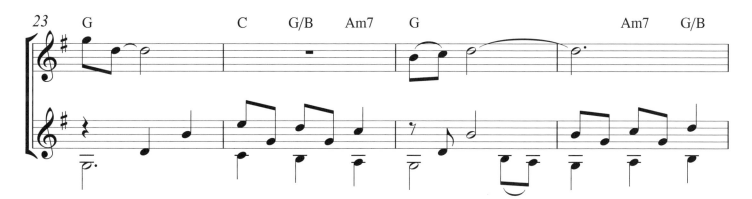

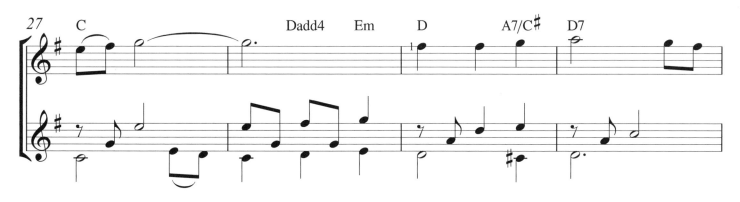

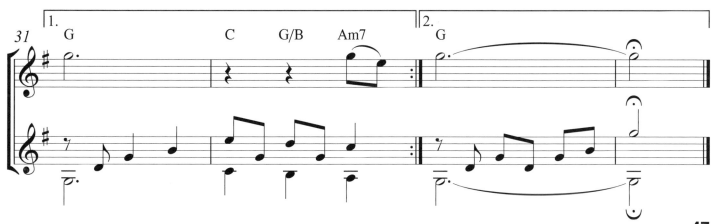

SOMEWHERE IN MY MEMORY

from the Twentieth Century Fox Motion Picture HOME ALONE
Words by Leslie Bricusse
Music by John Williams

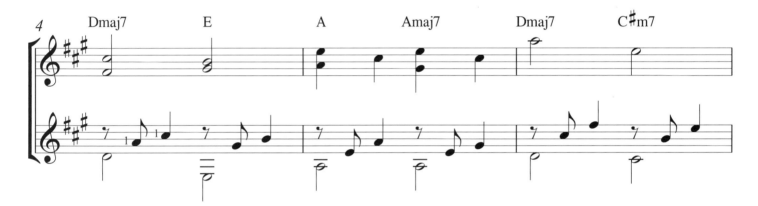

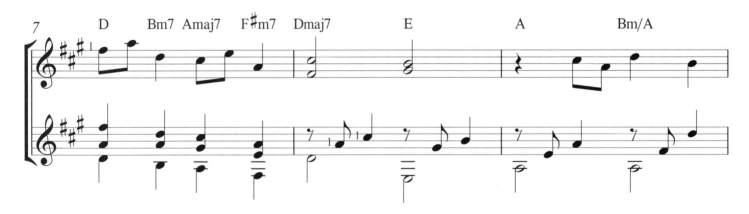

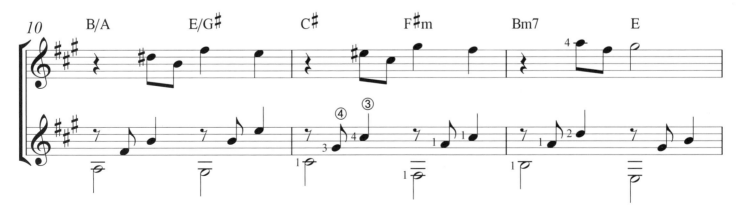

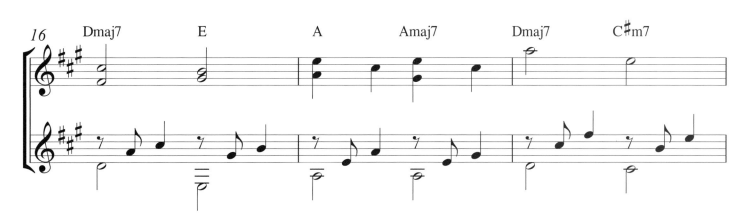

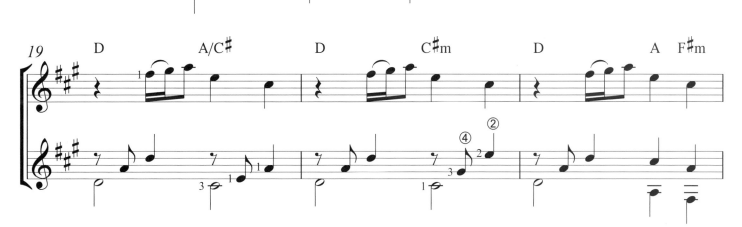

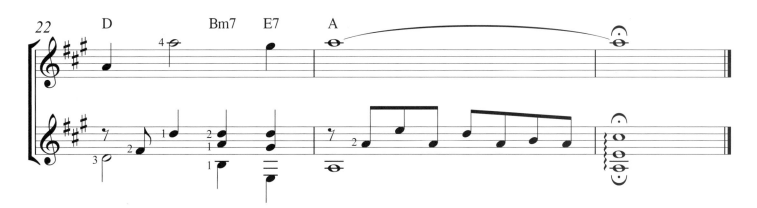

THIS CHRISTMAS

Words and Music by Donny Hathaway and Nadine McKinnor

*Play all chords with top note on 2nd string (unless otherwise indicated).

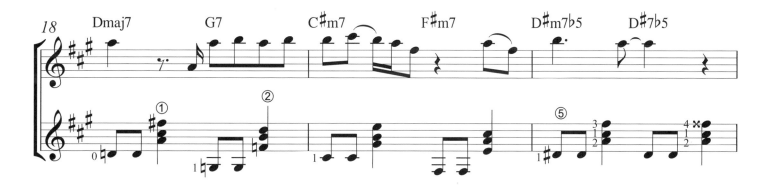

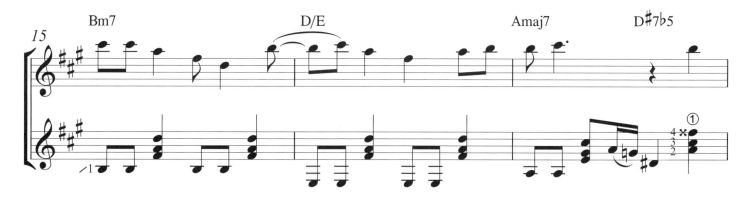

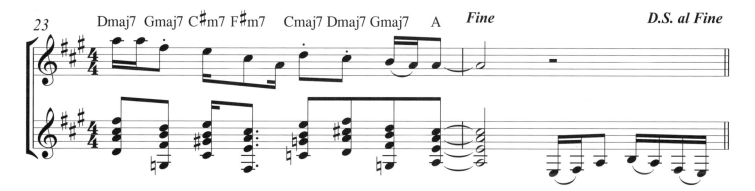

WHITE CHRISTMAS

Words and Music by Irving Berlin

Slowly, in 2

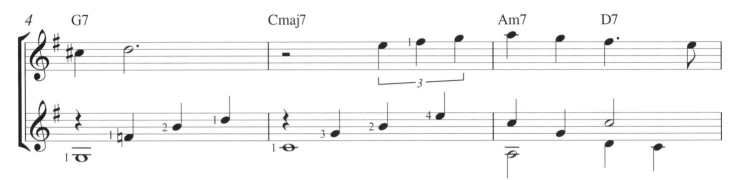

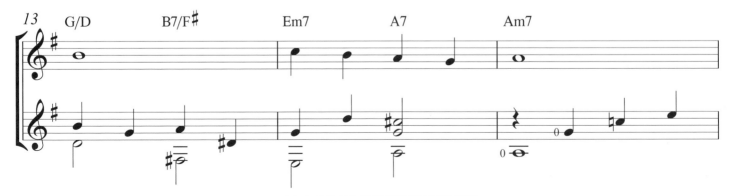

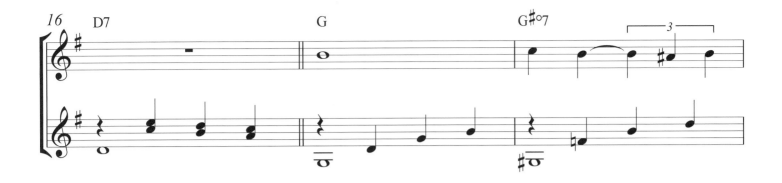

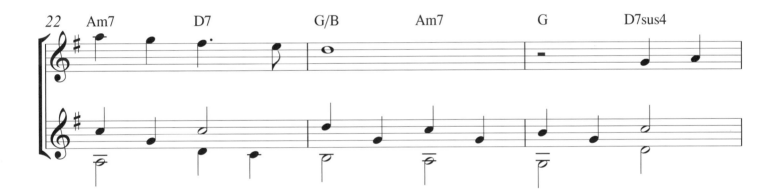

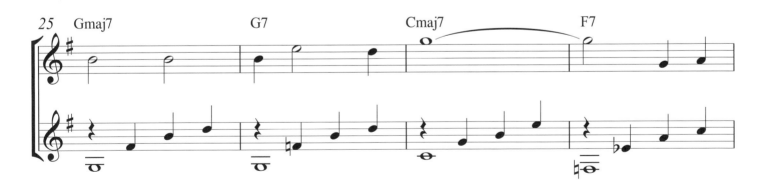

WINTER WONDERLAND

Words by Dick Smith
Music by Felix Bernard

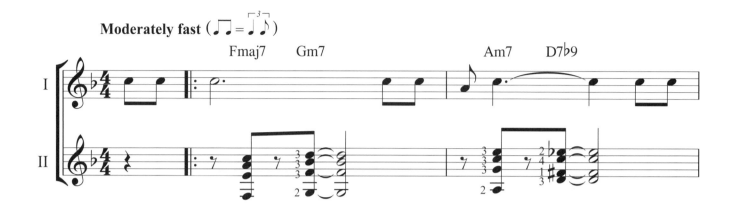

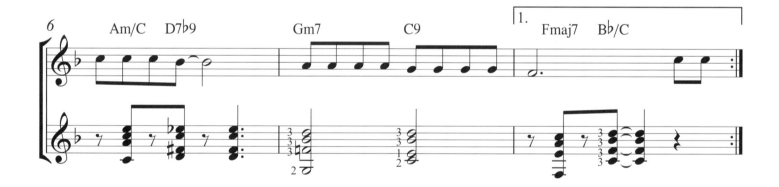

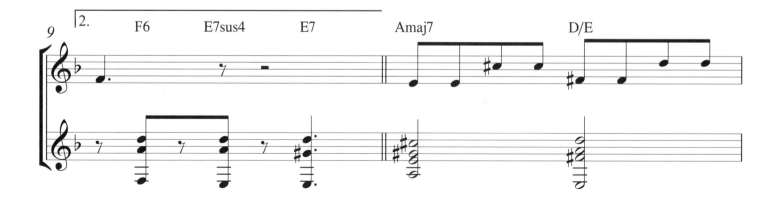

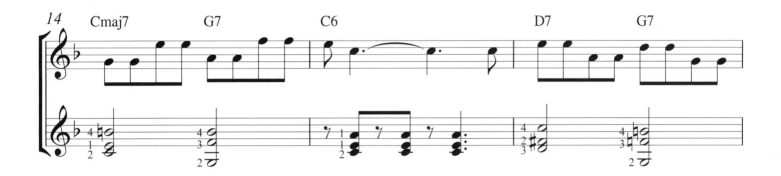

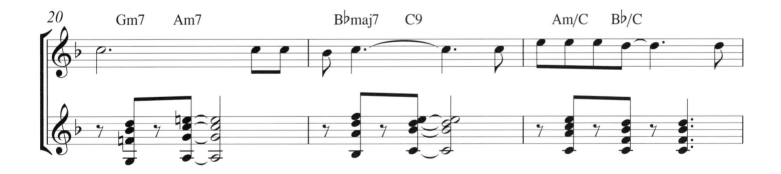

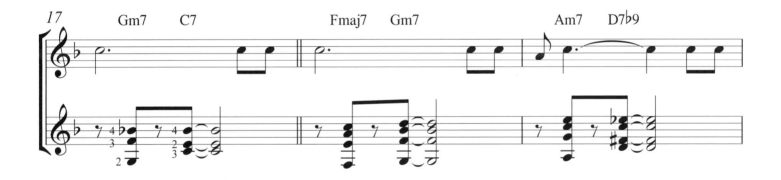

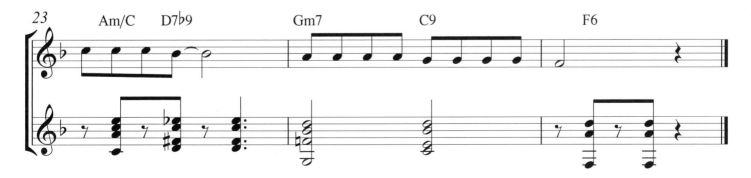

Celebrate Christmas
WITH YOUR GUITAR AND HAL LEONARD

THE BEST CHRISTMAS GUITAR FAKE BOOK EVER
INCLUDES TAB

Over 150 Christmas classics for guitar. Songs include: Blue Christmas • The Chipmunk Song • Frosty the Snow Man • Happy Holiday • A Holly Jolly Christmas • I Saw Mommy Kissing Santa Claus • I Wonder As I Wander • Jingle-Bell Rock • Rudolph, the Red-Nosed Reindeer • Santa Bring My Baby Back (To Me) • Suzy Snowflake • Tennessee Christmas • and more.
00240053 Melody/Lyrics/Chords $29.99

CHRISTMAS SONGS FOR EASY GUITAR

20 classic Christmas tunes: Blue Christmas • The Christmas Song (Chestnuts Roasting) • Frosty the Snow Man • Christmas Time Is Here • A Holly Jolly Christmas • I Saw Mommy Kissing Santa Claus • I'll Be Home for Christmas • Jingle-Bell Rock • Merry Christmas, Darling • Rudolph the Red-Nosed Reindeer • Silver Bells • You're All I Want for Christmas • and more.
00699804 Easy Guitar $9.99

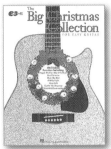

THE BIG CHRISTMAS COLLECTION FOR EASY GUITAR

Includes over 70 Christmas favorites, such as: Ave Maria • Blue Christmas • Deck the Hall • Feliz Navidad • Frosty the Snow Man • Happy Holiday • A Holly Jolly Christmas • Joy to the World • O Holy Night • Silver and Gold • Suzy Snowflake • and more. Does not include TAB.
00698978 Easy Guitar $19.99

FINGERPICKING CHRISTMAS SONGS
INCLUDES TAB

15 songs for intermediate-level guitarists, combining melody and harmony in superb fingerpicking arrangements: Baby, It's Cold Outside • Caroling, Caroling • Have Yourself a Merry Little Christmas • I Heard the Bells on Christmas Day • The Little Drummer Boy • Mary, Did You Know? • Mele Kalikimaka • Sleigh Ride • White Christmas • Wonderful Christmastime • and more.
00171333 Fingerstyle Guitar $10.99

CHRISTMAS CAROLS
For Easy Guitar

24 holiday favorites, including: Carol of the Bells • Good King Wenceslas • Hark! the Herald Angels Sing • I Saw Three Ships • Jingle Bells • Jolly Old St. Nicholas • O Come, O Come Immanuel • O Little Town of Bethlehem • Up on the Housetop • and more. Does not include TAB.
00702221 Easy Guitar $10.99

FINGERPICKING YULETIDE
INCLUDES TAB

Carefully written for intermediate-level guitarists, this collection includes an introduction to fingerstyle guitar and 16 holiday favorites: Do You Hear What I Hear • Happy Xmas (War Is Over) • A Holly Jolly Christmas • Jingle-Bell Rock • Rudolph the Red-Nosed Reindeer • and more.
00699654 Fingerstyle Guitar $12.99

CHRISTMAS CAROLS
Guitar Chord Songbook

80 favorite carols for guitarists who just need the lyrics and chords: Angels We Have Heard on High • Away in a Manger • Deck the Hall • Good King Wenceslas • The Holly and the Ivy • Irish Carol • Jingle Bells • Joy to the World • O Holy Night • Rocking • Silent Night • Up on the Housetop • Welsh Carol • What Child Is This? • and more.
00699536 Lyrics/Chord Symbols/ Guitar Chord Diagrams $14.99

FIRST 50 CHRISTMAS CAROLS YOU SHOULD PLAY ON GUITAR
INCLUDES TAB

Accessible, must-know Christmas songs are included in this collection arranged for guitar solo with a combo of tab, chords and lyrics. Includes: Angels We Have Heard on High • The First Noel • God Rest Ye Merry, Gentlemen • The Holly and the Ivy • O Christmas Tree • Silent Night • Up on the Housetop • What Child Is This? • and more.
00236224 Guitar Solo...........................$12.99

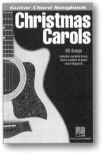

CLASSICAL GUITAR CHRISTMAS SHEET MUSIC

30 top holiday songs: Away in a Manger • Deck the Hall • Go, Tell It on the Mountain • Hallelujah Chorus • I Saw Three Ships • Jingle Bells • O Little Town of Bethlehem • Silent Night • The Twelve Days of Christmas • Up on the Housetop • We Wish You a Merry Christmas • What Child Is This? • and more. Does not include TAB.
00146974 Solo Classical Guitar $10.99

3-CHORD CHRISTMAS

You only need to know how to play 3 chords (G, C and D) on guitar to master these 25 holiday favorites: Away in a Manger • The Chipmunk Song • Frosty the Snow Man • Go, Tell It on the Mountain • Here Comes Santa Claus • Jingle Bells • The Little Drummer Boy • O Christmas Tree • Silent Night • Silver Bells • While Shepherds Watched Their Flocks • and more.
00146973 Guitar Solo...........................$10.99

CHRISTMAS JAZZ
INCLUDES TAB
Jazz Guitar Chord Melody Solos

21 songs in chord-melody style for the beginning to intermediate jazz guitarist in standard notation and tablature: Auld Lang Syne • Baby, It's Cold Outside • Cool Yule • Have Yourself a Merry Little Christmas • Mary, Did You Know? • Santa Baby • White Christmas • Winter Wonderland • and more.
00171334 Solo Guitar...........................$15.99

THE ULTIMATE GUITAR CHRISTMAS FAKE BOOK
INCLUDES TAB

200 Christmas standards: All I Want for Christmas Is You • Baby, It's Cold Outside • The Christmas Song (Chestnuts Roasting on an Open Fire) • Do You Want to Build a Snowman? • Feliz Navidad • Frosty the Snow Man • A Holly Jolly Christmas • Jingle Bells • Let It Snow! Let It Snow! Let It Snow! • Mary, Did You Know? • Rockin' Around the Christmas Tree • Santa Baby • Silent Night • What Child Is This? • White Christmas • and more.
00236446 Melody/Lyrics/Chords $29.99

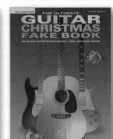

HAL•LEONARD®
www.halleonard.com